MW00967031

Hello out there!

ELECTRONIC COMMUNICATION

Chris Oxlade

Illustrated by
Colin Mier

W
FRANKLIN WATTS
A Division of Grolier Publishing
NEW YORK • LONDON • HONG KONG • SYDNEY
DANBURY, CONNECTICUT

© Franklin Watts 1997

First American Edition 1998 by
Franklin Watts, A Division of Grolier Publishing
90 Sherman Turnpike, Danbury, CT 06816

Oxlade, Chris.
    Electronic communication / Chris Oxlade.
        p.   cm. -- (Hello out there!)
    Includes index.
    Summary: Looks at the technology of communication from the
telegraph to fiber optics and the Internet. Includes a range of
follow-up activities.
        ISBN 0-531-14474-7
        1. Telecommunication--Juvenile literature.
    [1. Telecommunication. 2. Communication.] I. Title. II. Series.
    TK5102.4.092 1997
    621.382--dc21   97-1741
                                                                        CIP
                                                                        AC

Series editor: Rachel Cooke
Designer: Melissa Alaverdy
Picture acknowledgments:
Cover images: Telegraph Colour Library (background),
Steve Shott bl (with thanks to Orange PCS Ltd)
Robert Harding br.;
Corbis-Bettmann/UPI pp. 7b, 13, 24;
Mary Evans/Bruce Castle Museum p. 5; GEC-Marconi p. 15;
Robert Harding pp. 7t (Donald McLeish), 17 (FPG);
Hulton Getty p. 8; Image Bank pp. 25, 29t;
Nokia Communications pp. 29bl and br;
Rex Features p. 19; Science Photo Library p. 20 (Adam Hart-Davis);
Steve Shott p. 10, 23; Telegraph Colour Library p. 26.

Printed in Belgium

CONTENTS

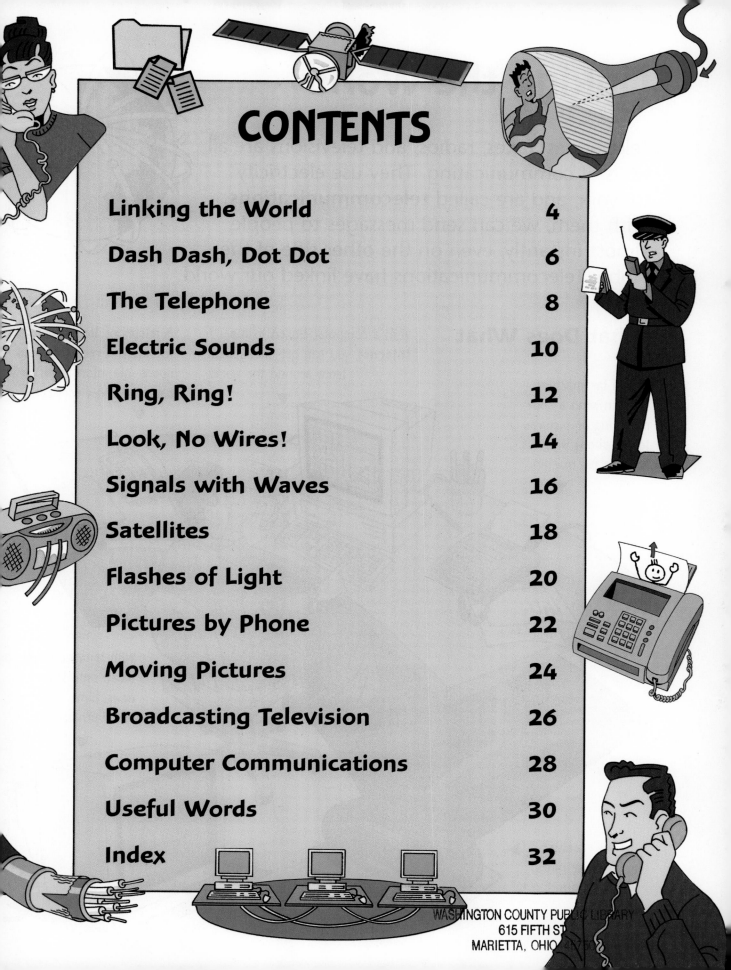

Linking the World

Telephones, faxes, radios, and televisions are all ways of communicating. They use electricity to work, and are called **telecommunications**. With them, we can send messages to people almost instantly, even on the other side of the globe. Telecommunications have linked our world.

What Does What

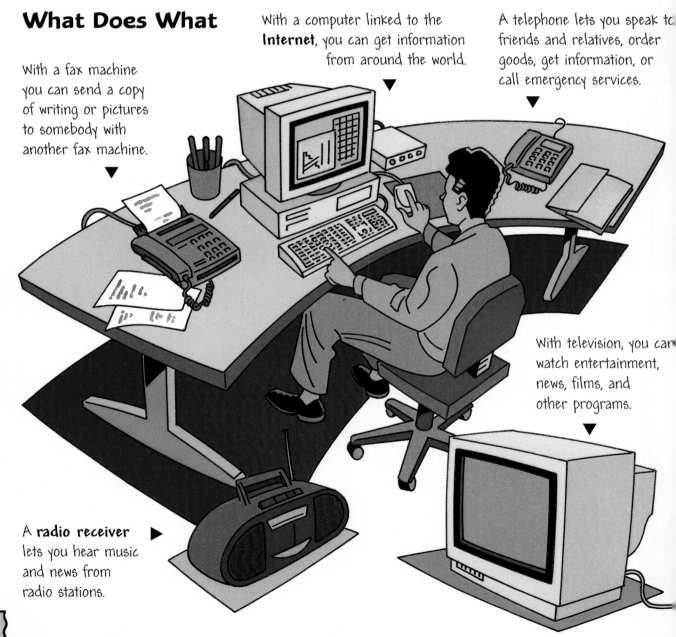

With a fax machine you can send a copy of writing or pictures to somebody with another fax machine.

With a computer linked to the **Internet**, you can get information from around the world.

A telephone lets you speak to friends and relatives, order goods, get information, or call emergency services.

With television, you can watch entertainment, news, films, and other programs.

A **radio receiver** lets you hear music and news from radio stations.

Before Electric Messages

The first electric telecommunications machine, called the **telegraph**, was invented in the early 1800s. Before then you could send a message by mail or by messenger. Until mail was carried by train in the 19th century, a letter would take several days to reach its destination.

HELLO!
The pigeon post (sending messages by pigeon) was devised around 2000 BC in what is now Iraq. A pigeon travelled over 300 miles (500 km) a day—far faster than a rider on horseback.

An 18th-century fast mail coach

Beacon to Beacon

Even in ancient times, a pre-arranged message could be sent very quickly over long distances. A line of bonfires, called beacons, were lit on hill tops so that each one could be seen by people at the next. When one person saw a blazing beacon, they lit their own.

A mechanical telegraph tower

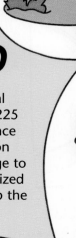

UP TO SPEED

In 1794, a line of mechanical telegraph stations 135 miles (225 km) long was built across France from Paris to Lille. Each station signaled a simple coded message to the next by moving its mechanized arms. A message could travel up the line in just a few minutes.

Dash Dash, Dot Dot

Railroad companies started using the telegraph in the 1840s to help keep their trains on time. Scientists had discovered that electricity could flow along wires and some engineers realized that they could use this to send messages. They sent the messages along wires in code by simply turning the electricity on and off, like flicking a light switch. The code used most was made up from dots and dashes—**Morse code**.

Morse code

a	·−	n	−·
b	−···	o	−−−
c	−·−·	p	·−−·
d	−··	q	−−·−
e	·	r	·−·
f	··−·	s	···
g	−−·	t	−
h	····	u	··−
i	··	v	···−
j	·−−−	w	·−−
k	−·−	x	−··−
l	·−··	y	−·−−
m	−−	z	−−··

Sending a Telegram Using Morse Code

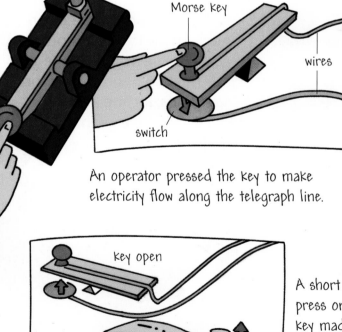

An operator pressed the key to make electricity flow along the telegraph line.

At the receiving machine, the electricity made a pen press against a moving roll of paper.

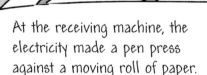

A short press on the key made a dot, and a long press made a dash.

When the key was released, the electricity stopped flowing and the pen stopped pressing.

The operator at the receiving end translated the code back into numbers and letters.

Telegram for Mr. Smith!

Until the middle of the 20th century, the telegraph was the only way most people could send a message quickly. They went to a telegraph office, where an operator sent their message to another office. A messenger took the message, called a telegram, to the person it was addressed to.

HELLO!
The cost of sending a telegraph message depended on the number of words used so people kept their messages very short!

A telegraph delivery boy of the 1920s.

UP TO SPEED

With a lot of practice, a telegraph operator could tap his or her key fast enough to send a message at 12 words a minute. How many words a minute can you manage?

Activity

Make this simple telegraph machine to send Morse messages. You can make the wires much longer so that the switch and bulb are in different rooms.

Battery

Lightbulb lights up when electricity flows

Press paper clip to send dots and dashes

Push pins

Wooden block

Wire

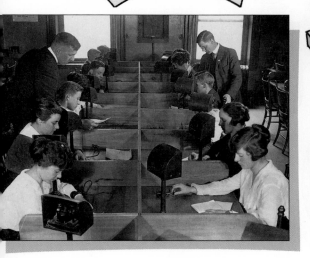

The Telephone

Pick up your telephone, press a few buttons and you can talk to your friends in another town—even in a different country. The telephone system needs the telephones themselves and a network that connects them all together.

An Accidental Invention

The telephone was invented in the United States in 1876 by Alexander Graham Bell. He was trying to make a new type of telegraph machine when he realized that it could send his voice as well as dots and dashes. The telephone was an instant success.

HELLO!

On many early telephones the earpiece and mouthpiece were the same. An instruction on one telephone read "Do not listen with your mouth and talk with your ear."

The man in the photograph is using a "candlestick" telephone —conveniently adapted! The other telephone is the earlier "butterstamp" telephone with the same earpieces and mouthpieces.

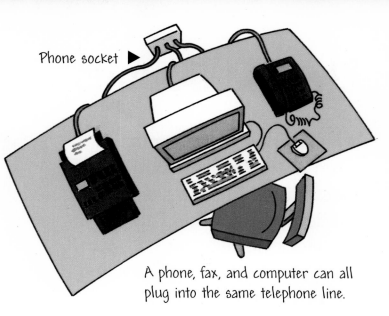

Phone, Fax, and Computer

The **telephone network** doesn't just carry telephone calls. Alongside them travel messages going between fax machines and between computers.

A phone, fax, and computer can all plug into the same telephone line.

Around the World

When the telephone was invented, there was no telephone network. But telephone companies quickly built **telephone exchanges** and telephone lines. Today, each country has its own network, linked to the networks of other countries, so that you can talk to people on the other side of the world.

Electric Sounds

A telephone carries your call from place to place with electricity, but your voice is made up of sound. The job of a telephone receiver is to turn your voice into electricity and to turn electricity back into sound that you can hear.

Earpiece —

Mouthpiece —

You listen to the earpiece. Inside is a tiny **loudspeaker** which turns electricity into sound. You speak into the mouthpiece. Inside is a **microphone** which turns sound into electricity.

What's in a Sound?

When you speak, you make the air around you vibrate. The tiny particles which make up the air get squashed together and then pulled apart as the sound moves by. Your ears detect these movements, which is why you can hear sound.

Air squashed together here ▼

Air pulled apart here ▼

Sound spreads out this way

Activity

You can see how vibrations make sound in a loudspeaker with this simple experiment.

Stand a cardboard tube on a piece of paper and draw around it. Cut out the circle and attach it to the end of the tube with sticky tape.

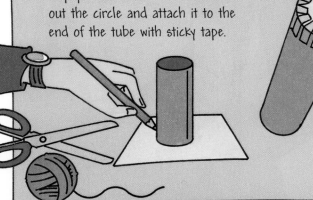

ound to Electricity

Want to know how a elephone receiver turns ound into electricity?

   The mouthpiece uses he sound of your voice to change the strength of an **electric current**, making t stronger or weaker. This changing current is called n **electrical signal**. It is an electrical copy of vibrations n the air. The electrical ignal is sent to the earpiece f another phone, where it s turned back into sound.

ierce a hole in the circle. Thread piece of string through the hole nd tie a knot in the end.

ut the tube to your ear and lide your fingers gently long the string.

What do ou hear?

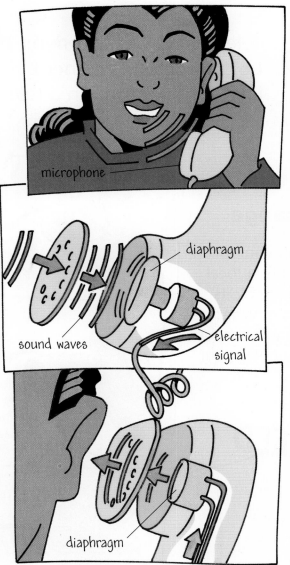

microphone

sound waves

diaphragm

electrical signal

diaphragm

The sound of your voice hits a microphone, which has an electric current flowing through it.

A **diaphragm** in the microphone moves up and down in the vibrating air. This changes the current, creating an electrical signal.

The electrical signal goes into an earpiece and is detected by a tiny electromagnet. This makes another diaphragm vibrate, recreating the sound.

Showing a Signal

You can draw an electrical signal made by a microphone as a wiggly line. As the line goes up, it means the electricity is getting stronger. As it comes back down, the electricity is getting weaker.

▲ strong current

weak current ▼

Ring, Ring!

Telephones can't work on their own. They have to be connected together before you can chat. This link is made through a telephone network.

At the Exchange

Each telephone in your local area is connected to a local telephone exchange by its own telephone line. When you dial your friend's number, the exchange connects your line to your friend's line.

The exchange detects that you have lifted your receiver.

Pressing numbers to dial connects the two lines and the exchange makes your friend's phone ring.

The exchange disconnects lines when you put your phone down.

UP TO SPEED

A large modern electronic telephone exchange can keep 100,000 telephone calls connected at the same time.

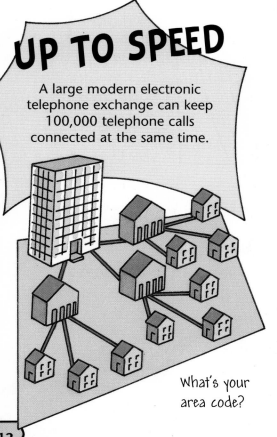

What's your area code?

Long-distance

But it's no good just being able to call people locally. So the different local exchanges are linked together over long distances. To call someone whose phone is connected to another exchange, you dial the code of that exchange, known as the area code, before the actual number.

This Way or That?

Your telephone call is carried between exchanges either by electrical cables, optical-fiber cables, or radio signals.

Number Please!

The first telephones had no buttons or dials. And telephone exchanges were worked by human operators. To make a call, you lifted your receiver and gave the operator the number you wanted. The operator made the connection by plugging in wires.

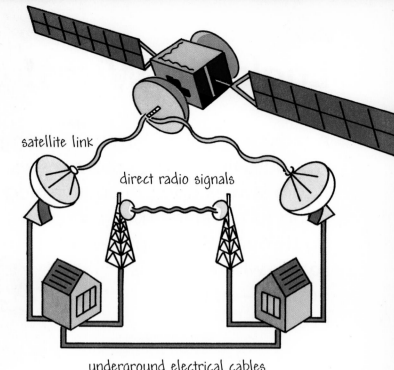

satellite link

direct radio signals

underground electrical cables or optical-fiber cable

HELLO!
The first automatic telephone exchange was invented by an American undertaker called Almon B. Strowger, who was fed up with getting wrong numbers.

Telephone operators making connections in a manual telephone exchange.

Look, No Wires!

A radio is a way of communicating without wires. It uses radio waves. **Radio waves** don't need anything thing to travel in. They can even go through the emptiness of space, where there is nothing—not even air!

Model boats, planes, and cars can be controlled by radio.

Using a Radio

Here's where radio is used in communications. . .

With a two-way radio you can talk to another person by radio. Emergency workers often use two-way radios.

Broadcast radio is for entertainment. A radio station sends out radio waves which anybody with a radio can pick up.

Radio waves sometimes carry telephone calls for part of their journey through the telephone network. A mobile telephone is linked to a network by radio.

UP TO SPEED

Radio waves carry messages at the speed of light—that's 300,000 km a second!

Making Radio Waves

Radio waves are made when an electrical signal goes along a wire. The waves spread out in all directions from the wire.

Radio-controlled plane

To a receiver

A machine that collects radio waves is called a receiver. It needs an aerial to detect the wave. The waves cause a tiny electrical signal in the aerial. Electronics in the receiver **amplify** the signal (make it bigger).

From a transmitter

Communications machines which make radio waves have a special wire called a **transmitter** where radio waves come from.

Activity

Try this simple experiment to make radio waves—and a crackling noise!

1 Hold one end of a long piece of wire against one terminal of a flashlight battery.

2 Put the wire near a radio which is turned on.

3 Brush the other end of the wire on the other terminal of the battery.

4 This should cause the wire to make radio waves, which you can hear as crackles on the radio.

HELLO!

The first person to use radio for communication was Guglielmo Marconi, from Italy. In 1901, he sent a Morse code message by radio from England across the Atlantic Ocean.

Signals with Waves

When radio takes the place of an electrical wire, what happens to the electrical signal that represents your voice and other sounds?

Instead of Wires

The answer is that a radio wave, called a carrier wave, is sent from one place to another instead of a wire. The electrical signal changes the shape of the **carrier wave** to make a radio signal. This is called **modulation**.

Wiggling Waves

You can think of a radio wave as a wave going along a rope or a ribbon when the end is wiggled. By changing how much, or how fast you wiggle the end, you can change the shape of the wave that moves along the rope.

A Few Useful Wave Words

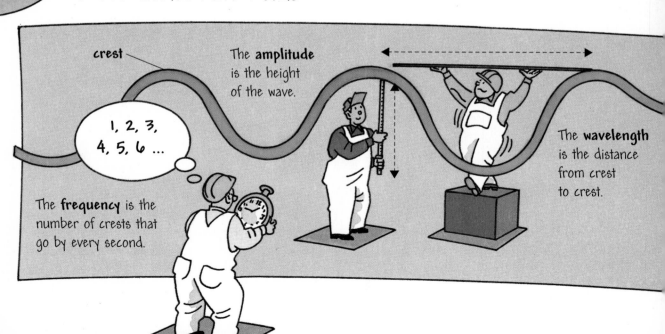

crest

The **amplitude** is the height of the wave.

1, 2, 3, 4, 5, 6 ...

The **wavelength** is the distance from crest to crest.

The **frequency** is the number of crests that go by every second.

Shaping the Waves!

Here are some simple diagrams to show how modulation happens. It's all done by electronic **circuits**. When the radio signals reach your radio, more circuits get the original electrical signal back. Amazingly, this is called demodulation!

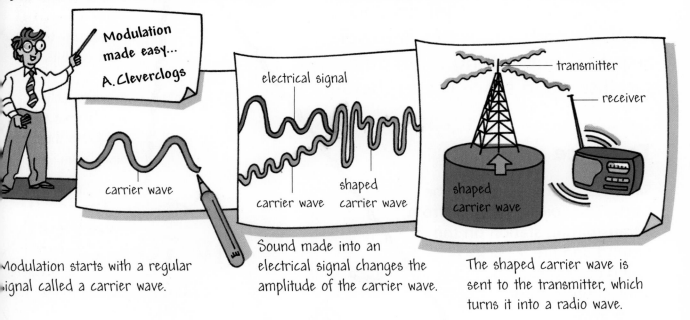

Modulation made easy...
A. Cleverclogs

carrier wave

electrical signal

carrier wave   shaped carrier wave

transmitter

receiver

shaped carrier wave

Modulation starts with a regular signal called a carrier wave.

Sound made into an electrical signal changes the amplitude of the carrier wave.

The shaped carrier wave is sent to the transmitter, which turns it into a radio wave.

Channels and Tuning

You can tune a radio in to hundreds of different radio stations. Each station sends out a signal using a carrier wave with a different frequency. When you tune your radio, you make the radio pick out the waves from the station you want to listen to.

Which station on which frequency is your radio usually tuned to?

Satellites

Radio is a great way of communicating. But sending radio signals long distances is tricky—hills get in the way and most radio signals can't curve around the Earth's surface. Transmitters and receivers on hill tops or tall towers help this, but putting them on a **satellite** up in space is even better.

Solar panels use sunlight to make electricity to power the satellite.

Antennas collect signals from Earth and beam them back down again.

To Space and Back

Satellites orbit high above the Earth. They pick up signals from a transmitting station on the ground and fire it back to a receiving station often thousands of miles away.

UP TO SPEED

A modern communications satellite can relay tens of thousands of telephone calls at the same time.

HELLO!

Early Bird, launched into space in 1965, was the first satellite to send regular live TV pictures. For the very first time, people could see events happening live on the other side of the world. In 1968, people in Europe watched live pictures of the Olympic Games in Mexico.

Phone from Anywhere

Many of the reports and pictures in your daily newspaper come from remote areas of the world where there are no telephones. They are sent directly to a satellite from a small portable dish carried by the reporter. In the future, everyday mobile phones will be able to talk directly to satellites, too.

Ahead of his time

Science-fiction writer Arthur C. Clarke was the brains behind the satellite idea. At the time, not even a rocket had been sent into space. It's 1945. . .

H'mmm. That's an idea!

$$\sqrt{72} + 3217$$
$$(462536$$
$$? = ??1?4$$
$$2 + 73164$$
$$11 \times 2 - 372$$
$$- 11 + 6721$$
$$= 22000$$

At 22,000 miles from Earth, a satellite in orbit would remain stationary over one spot as the Earth spins. . .

Just three satellites would cover the whole world!

What an idiot! We don't even know how to get into space yet!

Flashes of Light

Today, it's likely that when you make a long-distance telephone call, your call is carried between telephone exchanges not by electricity, but by **laser light**. The light travels along hair-thin glass threads called **optical fibers**.

Light coming out of optical fibers.

Inside an Optical Fiber

An optical fiber is not a hollow tube. It is made from solid glass, surrounded by a protective layer of plastic. The light whizzes through the glass, bouncing off the edges when it hits them.

optical fibers
in casing

cover

glass fiber

Light in Pulses

You can send Morse messages by making short and long flashes with a flashlight.

Coded flashes are used to send a telephone call along an optical fiber, too. The flashes are made with a laser that fires light along the fiber.

Activity

Here's how to make an optical fiber. It works just like the real thing, except that it's made of water instead of glass.

You will need a plastic soda bottle, a flashlight, and some water.

1. Ask an adult to cut a small hole halfway up the bottle.

3. Light bounces along curved water jet.

2. Shine a flashlight into the water from behind the hole.

converter

Ons and Offs

UP TO SPEED

Using complex electronic circuits to control the pulses of light, 10,000 telephone calls can travel along a hair-thin optical fiber all at the same time.

The light code used in an optical fiber is not Morse code, but it is made up of ons and offs. Just as a radio wave is modulated (has its shape changed) by the electrical signal it is sending, the flashes of light which travel along an optical fiber are controlled by the electrical signal it is sending.

The telephone turns our voices into an electrical signal (see page 11). Here's how an electrical signal is turned into a signal of light:

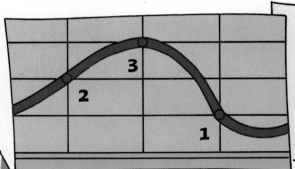

Electronic circuits keep measuring the amplitude of the signal.

2 ▶ **10**	Each measurement is turned into a binary number. A binary number has only 0s and 1s in it.
3 ▶ **11**	
1 ▶ **01**	

Because the signal is now made up of 0s and 1s, we call it a **digital signal**.

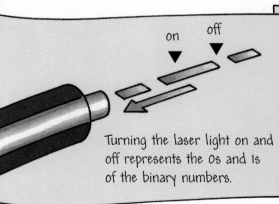

on   off

Turning the laser light on and off represents the 0s and 1s of the binary numbers.

optical signal

The binary numbers are sent one by one along the optical fiber.

When the flashes arrive, they are turned back into the original electrical signal which goes to the telephone.

converter

electrical signal

Pictures by Phone

HELLO!

The fax is older than you probably think. The first fax was sent in 1907 between Munich and Berlin. At the time, the fax was called telephotography.

A telephone receiver turns sound into an electrical signal which can travel through the telephone network. A fax machine turns writing and pictures into an electrical signal. So with a fax machine, you can send writing and pictures through the telephone network.

Patterns to Signals

This is how an image is sent from one fax machine to another:

1. Rollers make a sheet of paper move slowly through the machine.

The fax is sent from this machine.

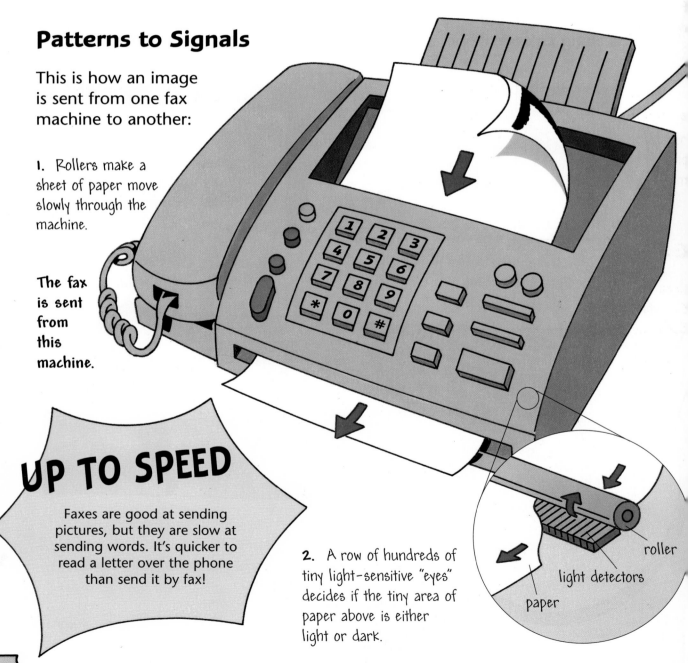

UP TO SPEED

Faxes are good at sending pictures, but they are slow at sending words. It's quicker to read a letter over the phone than send it by fax!

2. A row of hundreds of tiny light-sensitive "eyes" decides if the tiny area of paper above is either light or dark.

roller

light detectors

paper

3. The information is sent along the telephone line.

Fax being received

4. Rollers feed heat-sensitive paper into the machine.

5. Information from the telephone line controls row of tiny heaters, one for each "eye" in the sending fax machine.

heating elements

6 An electrical message of a dark area turns a heater on. Under the heaters that are on, the paper turns black to make a dot. Gradually, the picture is made up and rolls out of the receiving fax machine.

Going Square

Look at a fax with a magnifying glass. Can you see the tiny squares? Each square is a dot.

fax copy

Each square is made by the fax's heat-sensitive eyes. This picture shows how a photograph would come out after being faxed.

original photograph

Moving Pictures

Television is a way of seeing things as they happen somewhere else. Of all the kinds of communication, television has the most effect on our lives. It entertains us, informs us, and keeps us in touch with the rest of the world.

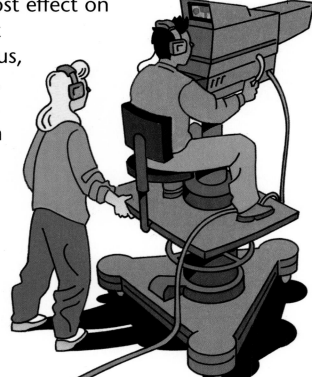

TV camera

An electrical signal is sent to the TV transmitter.

Television Cameras

The job of a television camera is to take an electronic picture of a scene. It turns the patterns of color in the scene into an electrical signal. As the scene changes, so does the electronic picture, and so the electrical signal. So the signal represents a moving picture.

HELLO!

Television started in the United States and Europe in the 1930s. At first, there were only one or two programs a day. All the programs were in black and white. Color came in the 1960s.

Early TVs were very large but had very small screens!

Television Sets

A television set turns an electrical signal back into a moving picture. Here's what the inside of a television set looks like.

1. Beams of tiny particles called **electrons** are fired from the back of the tube. The strength of the beam is controlled by the electrical signal.

Inside the television is a glass tube. The screen you look at is at one end of the tube.

The lines are made up so fast that the eye cannot see them—we just see the complete picture.

2. The beams zigzag across the back of the screen, making the picture line by line.

3. The beams make the back of the screen glow where they hit it.

At a TV Station

The signals that your television receives and turns into pictures come from a television station. At first most programs were live but now many are recorded on video tape—this gives the program makers a chance to take out any mistakes! But live programs, such as the news, are still **broadcast**.

In a live program, the signals from the different cameras in the studio go to a control room. Here, they are mixed with sound, graphics, (such as a logo) and other pictures to make up the picture which is broadcast.

Broadcasting Television

You know that a television camera makes a signal, and that a television set turns it back into a moving picture. But how does the signal get from a television station to your home, perhaps hundreds of miles away?

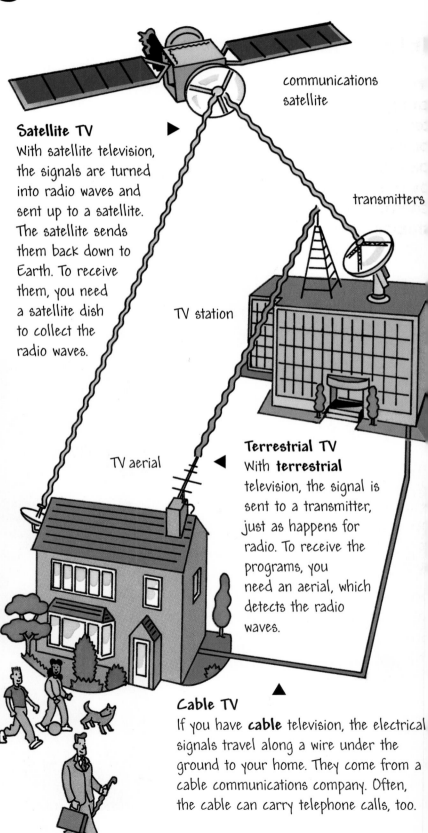

Satellite TV
With satellite television, the signals are turned into radio waves and sent up to a satellite. The satellite sends them back down to Earth. To receive them, you need a satellite dish to collect the radio waves.

communications satellite

transmitters

TV station

TV aerial

Terrestrial TV
With **terrestrial** television, the signal is sent to a transmitter, just as happens for radio. To receive the programs, you need an aerial, which detects the radio waves.

Cable TV
If you have **cable** television, the electrical signals travel along a wire under the ground to your home. They come from a cable communications company. Often, the cable can carry telephone calls, too.

A TV and radio transmitter tower. The dishes attached transmit the signals from mobile phones.

Interactive Viewing

Interactive television means that you can send information back to the television company as well as receive programs. You might be able to take part in programs, such as quiz shows, by pressing buttons on your remote control, or order things from special shopping television channels.

Digital TV will give a new meaning to "channel surfing"!

Going Digital

Do you remember what *digital* means (see page 21)? Well, digital TV means TV which comes to your TV as digital signals. In the future, digital TV will be the standard system. Hundreds of digital signals can be sent at once and still use radio signals, cables, or satellites.

UP TO SPEED

A transmitter, a cable, or a satellite can handle many more digital signals than normal signals. When digital television arrives, early in the twenty-first century, there will be hundreds and hundreds of channels to choose from.

Computer Communications

Computers can do almost anything, so you won't be surprised to hear that they can communicate with each other, too. This means that information stored on one computer can be looked at by another computer, even if the two computers are on opposite sides of the world!

Small Networks

All the computers in this office are linked together to make a network to share company information. The links are made with wires stretching from one computer to the next.

... and BIG Networks

Computers can also exchange information over the telephone. Each computer needs a device called a **modem**, to connect it to the telephone network.

modem

The Internet

The Internet is easily the world's biggest computer network. Tens of millions of computers are linked to it. But what can you do on the Internet?

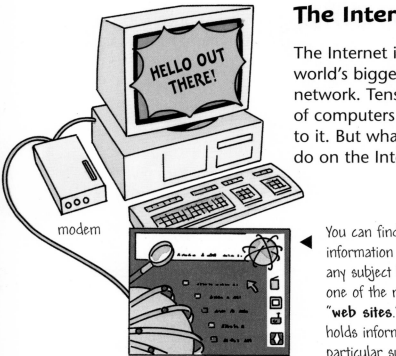

modem

You can send and receive messages. The message is called an e-mail (short for electronic mail).

You can find information on almost any subject by visiting one of the millions of "**web sites.**" Each one holds information on a particular subject.

You can send any information from your computer to any other computer on the Internet.

Computer Conferencing

With a **video** camera linked to a computer, people can have a meeting without having to be in the same room, or even the same country. They talk and see each other over the computer network. This is called **video conferencing**.

HELLO!
People are already using video conferencing. In the future, they might also use virtual conferencing, where they will be able to see computer models of other people, talk to them, and even touch them.

This is a video conference. The person on the screen can see the people in the room via the computer and the small video camera on top of it.

UP TO SPEED

A portable digital assistant (PDA for short) is a portable telephone, fax machine, digital diary and address book, and a personal computer. All this in a machine that fits in your pocket. You can store people's details on it, phone them, fax them, send them e-mail, and surf the Internet—wherever you are in the world. What do you think Alexander Graham Bell would think of that?

A PDA open: a personal organizer, fax, and link to the Internet.

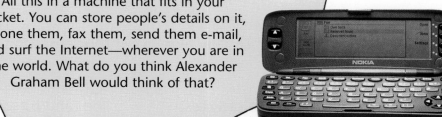

A PDA closed: mobile phone.

Useful Words

amplify: to make the amplitude of an electrical signal bigger, making a weak signal into a strong signal.

amplitude: the height of a wave.

broadcast: to send a radio or TV signal to many different receivers at the same time.

cable television: a way of receiving TV pictures along cables under the ground (rather than by aerials or satellites).

carrier wave: a regular signal whose shape is changed to send electrical signals by radio.

circuit: an arrangement of wires and electronic components that an electric current flows around.

diaphragm: a thin, flat metal disc which vibrates when sound hits it, or vibrates to make sound.

digital signal: an electrical signal which is made up of ons and offs rather than a constantly changing signal.

digital television: a TV system which sends its signals in digital form.

electric current: the flow of tiny particles called electrons, usually along a metal wire.

electrical cable: a bundle of wires.

electrical signal: an electric current that keeps changing in strength to represent something, such as a sound.

electromagnet: a coil of wire that becomes a magnet when an electric current flows through it.

electron: one of the tiny particles which make up an atom. Electrons also make up an electric current.

frequency: the number of wave crests which pass a point every second.

interactive television: a television system which lets the viewer send information to the television station to choose what pictures to see.

Internet: the huge network of computers linked together, stretching right around the world.

laser: a device that makes a very bright, narrow beam of light called a laser beam.

loudspeaker: an electronic device that turns an electrical signal into sound.

microphone: an electrical device that turns sound into an electrical signal.

modem: short for modulator/demodulator. A modem turns computer data into signals which can travel down a telephone line (and turns them back again).

modulation: using an electrical signal to change a radio wave or a beam of light so that it can carry another signal.

Morse code: a code of long and short pulses of electricity, light or sound which represents letters and numbers.

optical fiber: a thin glass or plastic fiber along which light travels without escaping.

radio receiver: an electronic device that detects radio signals and turns them into sounds.

radio signal: a radio wave that keeps changing shape so that it can carry a signal from one place to another.

radio wave: a type of wave called an electromagnetic wave that is a bit like light (except that it is invisible).

satellite: an artificial object that orbits the Earth in space.

telecommunications: all the types of communication that work using electricity (telephones, fax, computers, television, and radio).

telegraph: an electric communication system that uses on and off codes (such as Morse code) to represent letters and numbers.

telephone exchange: a building where all the telephones in an area are connected together and also connected to other telephone exchanges.

telephone network: the network of telephones, telephone wires, telephone exchanges, cables, and communication satellites.

terrestrial television: a way of receiving TV pictures by radio waves travelling through the Earth's atmosphere.

transmitter: an aerial that sends out radio waves.

tune: to adjust a radio or television receiver to pick out just the signals from the station you want to see or listen to.

video: any sort of moving picture, or a way of recording moving pictures.

video conferencing: talking to people on the telephone and seeing a television picture of them at the same time.

wavelength: the distance between two crests of a wave.

web site: a store of information on a particular subject area held on a computer linked into the "world-wide web" or Internet. Any other computer in the web can visit a web site, display its contents on screen, and take information from it.

Index